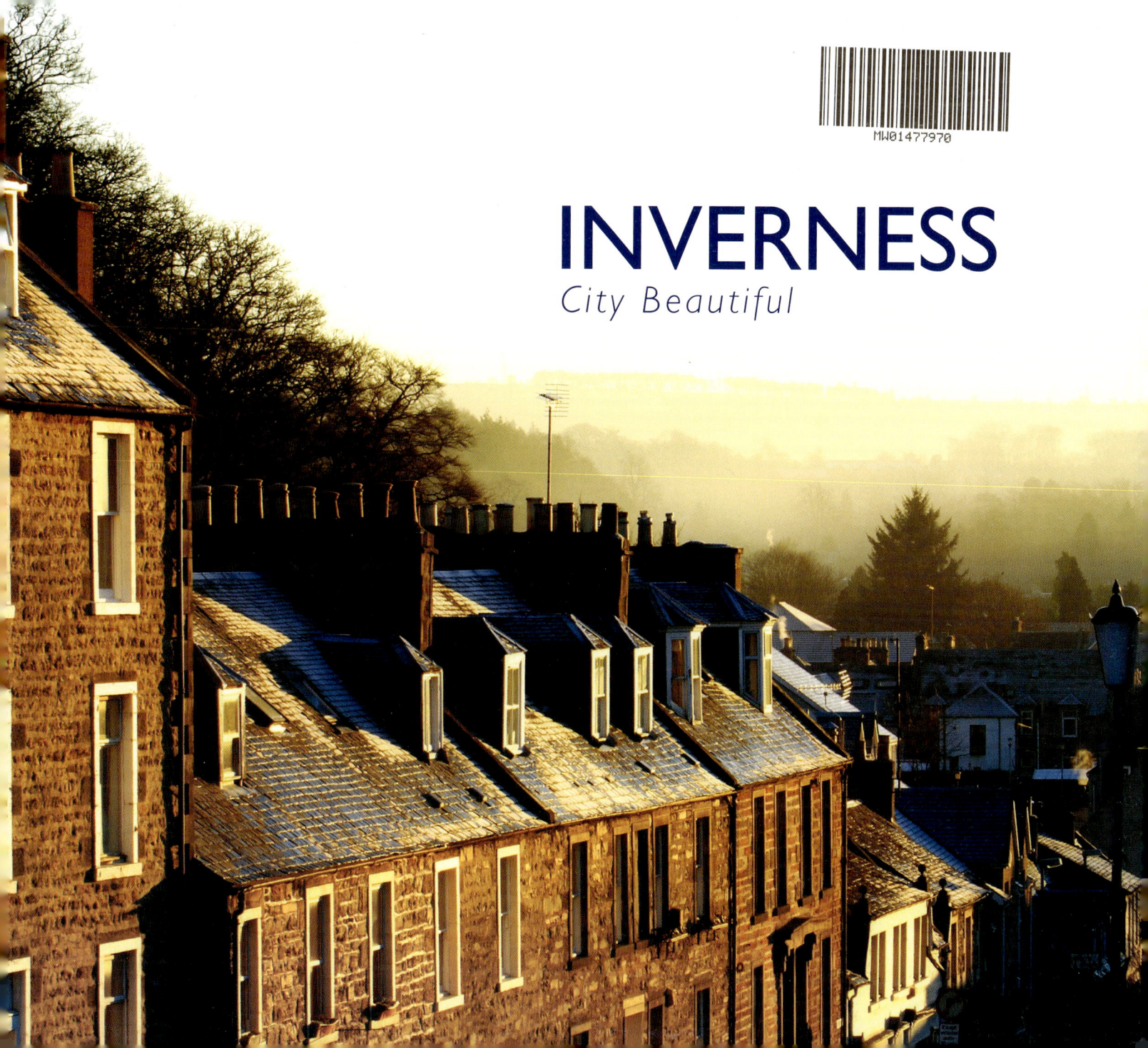

First published in Great Britain in 2010 by
The Derby Books Publishing Company Limited
3 The Parker Centre,
Derby, DE21 4SZ.

© Jack Watson, 2010.

All Rights Reserved. No part of this publication may be reproduced, stored in a retrieval system, or transmitted in any form, or by any means, electronic, mechanical, photocopying, recording or otherwise without the prior permission in writing of the copyright holders, nor be otherwise circulated in any form or binding or cover other than in which it is published and without a similar condition being imposed on the subsequent publisher.

A catalogue record for this book is available from the British Library.

Previous page: A winter scene of View Place from Inverness Castle.

ISBN 978-1-85983-785-6

Printed and bound by Progress Press, Malta.

Jack Watson

INVERNESS
City Beautiful

Contents

Foreword	6
Introduction	7
Pre-history	8
The City Centre	12
The River Ness	59
Inverness Castle	71
Battle of Culloden	74
Caledonian Canal	83
Loch Ness	92
Parks and Leisure	102
Inverness Caledonian Thistle	112
Surrounding Area	114

Foreword

Inverness is one of Europe's fastest-growing cities, celebrated for its culture, history and exceptional beauty, so when I was offered the chance to photograph and write about such a beautiful part of the world there was absolutely no way I could refuse. As a photographer, I have had the pleasure of capturing all that is wonderful about the most northerly city in the United Kingdom and, with Inverness being my hometown, I really couldn't have landed a more exciting assignment. That said, like any worthwhile project it has not been all plain sailing, with plenty of late-night research sessions and some fairly unpredictable Highland weather to keep me entertained. Thankfully, I have had some excellent guidance from the staff at DB Publishing who have been brilliant throughout. I am also fortunate enough to have had a great deal of support and encouragement from family and friends and for all this I am extremely grateful. I hope that the reader will enjoy this book and learn something along the way about the beautiful and historic city of Inverness.

Special thanks and love to
Wendy, Cuillin, Mum, Andy, Nannie, Morag, Tom, Ann, Robert and Gordon.

Thanks also to:
Am Baile (www.ambaile.org.uk)
and
The National Trust for Scotland (www.nts.org.uk)
for providing information regarding some of the locations featured in this book.

Inverness, City Beautiful is dedicated to the memory of
Jackie Moffat Watson and Nigel Thomson Sutherland

Introduction

The ancient settlement of Inverness is often referred to as the capital of the Highlands and latterly, due to its numerous 'Britain in Bloom' successes, it has also come to be known as the Flower Capital. Inverness, meaning mouth of the Ness, reference to its geographical position, is steeped in history and although its date of origin is unknown, the surrounding area is thought to have first been occupied in around 3500 BC when the Neolithic people introduced farming to the land. Important as a bridge-point over the River Ness, Inverness was a chief stronghold of the Picts, with King Brude understood to have been residing at a vitrified fort on Craig Phadrig hill. It is believed that St Columba, the Gaelic missionary monk, met with King Brude in AD 565 in a bid to convert the Pictish King to Christianity. St Columba's visit to Inverness also links him with the Old High Church on Bank Street, and an encounter with the Loch Ness Monster!

After killing King Duncan in 1040 Macbeth (1005–1057) is thought to have inhabited the original castle, which stood on the Auld Castlehill about 1km north-east of the present-day site. Around the mid-12th century Inverness secured its status as a royal burgh on the strength of its growing importance as a trading port. Furs, hides, wool and timber were all exported as far afield as the Mediterranean. As a result Inverness prospered economically and became the most important northern outpost. This, however, made it a prime target for attack, and during the Wars of Independence in the 13th century, Inverness was also a regular target for both English and Scottish armies. The last battle on British soil was fought at Culloden Moor a few miles east of Inverness. On 16 April 1746, Bonnie Prince Charlie led the starving and out-numbered Jacobites to defeat against the Hanoverians in a battle which was over in less than an hour. The statue of Flora Macdonald in front of Inverness Castle is a reminder of this bloody conflict.

The 19th century shows a more industrious side to the city with the building of the Royal Northern Infirmary in 1803, followed by the Caledonian Canal in 1822 to link east and west Scotland. The 1830s saw a new castle being built. The railway became a reality for Inverness in 1855 bringing with it the all-important tourism industry, which Inverness still very much relies on today. St Andrew's Cathedral was built in 1869 and in 1882 the present-day Town House was completed. All this helped to strengthen Inverness's place as the capital of the Highlands.

Twentieth-century Inverness showed continued growth, with industries such as distilling, shipbuilding, wool milling and engineering boosting the local economy. Oil, construction and timber trades now take precedence along with health services, administration and notably tourism which was greatly aided by the Highland Year of Culture in 2007 that saw record numbers flock to the Highland capital to soak up its unique atmosphere. The 21st century has seen Inverness gain city status and, with the regeneration of the Old Town, this beautiful part of the world should continue to thrive and provide much enjoyment for generations to come.

Pre-history

A section of the stone circle that surrounds the south-west cairn.

The central ring cairn showing the large stone kerbing that can be seen on the inside and outside of all the cairns.

One of the stones surrounding the north-east passage cairn.

Balnuaran of Clava

Clava Cairns is one of the best-preserved Bronze Age burial sites in Scotland. Located a few miles east of Inverness lie three cairns surrounded by stone circles that are thought to date from between 1500 and 2000 BC. There are many sites like this in the Inverness area, but this one is by far the most impressive. The three cairns sit in line, with the north-east cairn and south-west cairn being passage cairns and the central cairn being an enclosed ring. The outside cairn's passageways align with the midwinter sun and all the cairns have large stone kerbing on the inside and outside. Although not a lot is known about the people who built these tombs, it is understood that very few people were buried here and that perhaps the burial tombs were reserved for the elite. Even less is known about the stones that encircle the cairns although some believe they may have been added at a later date.

Sadly a road was built through the stone circle at the south-west passage cairn, leaving one stone marooned.

Craig Phadrig is seen here from Inverness Castle with the River Ness in the foreground.

This gap in the trees reminds us that before Craig Phadrig was covered by forest, it must have made a tremendous lookout point.

Craig Phadrig

Craig Phadrig is a wooded hill that dominates the skyline above Inverness. Located three miles west of the city centre, it is the site of a vitrified Iron Age fort, which consists of two grass-covered ramparts. It is also reputed to be where Christian missionary St Columba spoke with Pictish chief King Brude in the sixth century. The fort is thought to have been built between the fourth and fifth century BC and occupied by the Picts from around 500 to AD 700. Its remains were first examined in the 18th century by John Williams, a local mining engineer, who said 'At the distant period, when the hill was actually a fort or a citadel, its aspect and surroundings must have been somewhat different from what they are at present. It must have been a bare, barren hill, capable of overlooking the whole country, carefully guarded to serve as a place of retreat, and ready at any moment to be put into a state of defences.' At 169 metres high Craig Phadrig hill would certainly have been an impressive look-out point. Today the hill makes for a lovely forest walk with stunning views over the Beauly Firth.

As you approach the ramparts of the fort the walk steepens.

City Centre

Inverness has a picturesque city centre packed with interesting attractions including a selection of historic architecture. With Inverness's oldest complete house, Church Street is an excellent place to start.

Church Street

The streets of Inverness have seen a fair amount of regeneration in recent times with new paving and artwork throughout the city.

An example, on Church Street, of stone artwork illuminated at night, highlighting inspirational words carved out in both Gaelic and English.

Abertarff House

Located halfway up Church Street, Abertarff House was built in 1593 and is the oldest surviving house in Inverness. It was the town house of Colonel Archibald Fraser of Beaufort and Abertarff, who was the son of Lord Lovat of the '45 rebellion. It remained Fraser property until it was acquired in the mid-19th century by the National Commercial Bank of Scotland. In 1966 the National Trust for Scotland gave this fine example of Scots domestic architecture a new lease of life with a timely restoration.

Old High Church

The Old High Church overlooks the River Ness and is the oldest church in Inverness. It rests on St Michael's Mount, where St Columba of Iona is said to have preached.

The Old High Church was used as a prison for Jacobite soldiers following the Battle of Culloden; prisoners were subsequently executed in the church graveyard.

The Old High Church has been Celtic, Roman Catholic, Episcopalian and Presbyterian in its long and eventful history.

Old Gaelic Church

The Old Gaelic Church was built in 1649 and is located at the far end of Church Street. In the aftermath of the 1715 rebellion it provided a place of worship for Gaelic-speaking Government troops who were garrisoned in the area and could not attend the Old High Church. In 1792 the church was rebuilt and in 1822 further reconstruction work took place. Gas lighting was installed in 1827 allowing the church to hold the town's first regular English-spoken evening services.

In 1954 the Revd Ewan MacQueen and his congregation bought the Gaelic Church. Consequently the building was briefly renamed the MacQueen Memorial Church until 1958, when the congregation joined the Free Church of Scotland and the building became known as Greyfriars Free Church. The Old Gaelic Church was sold in 1994 and is now a second-hand book shop and cafe.

Dunbar's Hospital

Dunbar's Hospital was built in 1668 by Provost Alexander Dunbar, replacing an earlier hospital. It is thought that it was constructed using materials from Cromwell's demolished citadel; a fort built between 1652 and 1658 during Cromwell's administration. The building comprises three storeys and has been used for a range of purposes over the years. The right-hand section of the ground floor was used as a Grammar School up until 1792, when the Inverness Royal Academy was built.

The left-hand section of the ground floor was used as a weighhouse. Evidence of this can be seen above the arched doorway on the Dunbar coat-of-arms, which has an inscription that declares that the rent of the weigh-house will be payable to the hospital's treasurer.

Bow Court

Bow Court can be found on the corner of Church Street and School Lane. It was built in 1722 on land gifted by Lady Drummuir to house two families and a trades hall.

Bow Court was restored in 1972 by William Glashan to be used as flats.

Bridge Street

At the south end of Church Street lies Bridge Street, which connects Inverness High Street with the Ness Bridge.

Preservation of the Gaelic language can be seen throughout the city centre in the form of bilingual signage.

The Steeple

The Town Steeple sits on the corner of Church Street and Bridge Street. It was completed to the designs of William Sibbald in 1791 at a total cost of £3,400. The steeple, which replaced an earlier tolbooth and prison, is 130ft high and was severely damaged by an earthquake in 1816. It was left twisted and, although eventually repaired, it became something of an attraction as it tilted to give Inverness its version of the Leaning Tower of Pisa.

The Gellions bar

Around halfway down Bridge Street, you will find The Gellions bar. Established in 1841, it is Inverness's oldest public house. The Gellions is popular with both locals and tourists and with regular live music it is well worth a visit.

The Museum

Inverness Museum and Art Gallery can be found just off Bridge Street on Castle Wynd. Inverness's first museum was opened in 1826 for the promotion of Science and Literature with its collections inherited by the current museum which was founded in 1880. There is plenty to see in the museum including Devonian fossil fishes, prehistoric archaeology, Pictish symbol stones, Jacobite memorabilia and Inverness silver. The museum reopened in 2007, following a refurbishment for the Highland Year of Culture, with a range of new displays and visitor facilities.

Bridge Street meets Bank Street and the River Ness.

Bank Street

Bank Street and the River Ness from the Ness Bridge looking north.

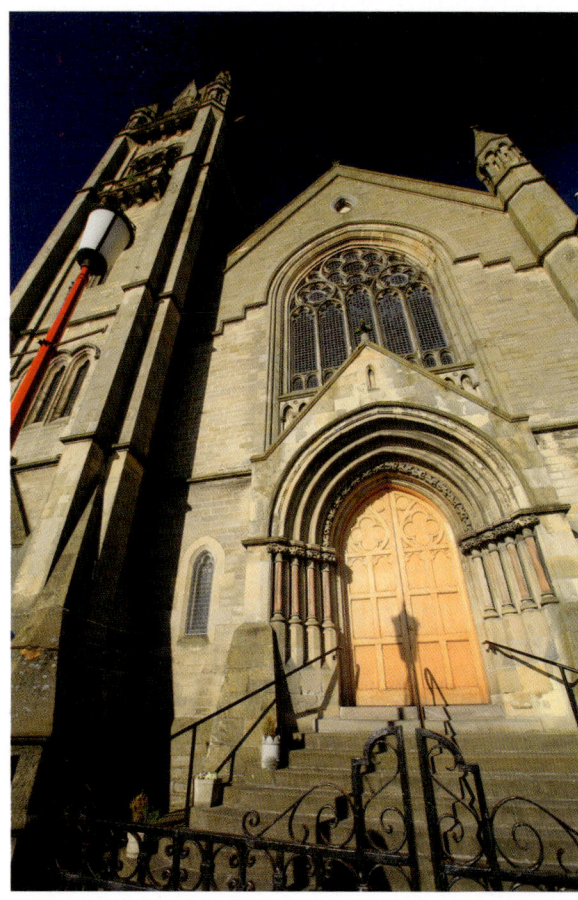

Free North Church
The Free North Church on Bank Street was built in 1893 after its congregation outgrew its previous building on North Lane.

Seen here from the Greig Street Bridge, the Free North Church is easily identified by having the tallest spire of the riverside churches.

Church Lane

To the left of the Free North Church is Church Lane, which connects Bank Street with Church Street.

This view is towards Dunbar Hospital from a well-lit Church Lane.

The regeneration of Inverness's streets has left a trail of thought-provoking writings dotted throughout city. This is one example that can be seen on Church Lane.

St Columba High Church

St Columba High Church was built in 1852 on the site of an old brewery, in Perpendicular Gothic style, by MacKenzie and Matthews.

St Columba's was badly damaged by a fire in 1940, but was later restored by the voluntary work of members of the congregation.

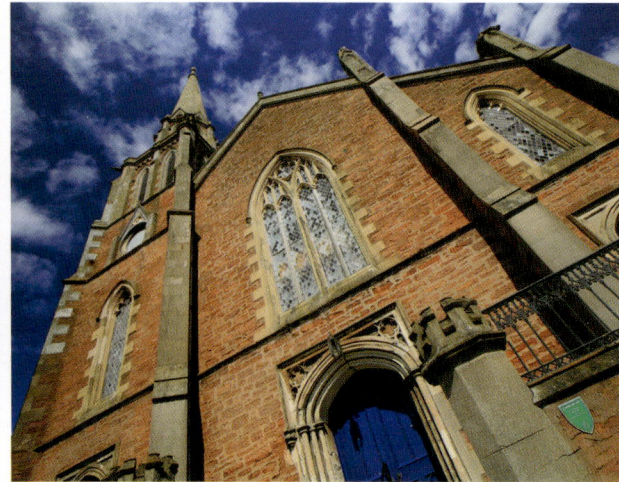

The Inverness Courier

Established in 1817, *The Inverness Courier* is the city's oldest newspaper.

The bi-weekly newspaper currently occupies New Century House, which was built in 2001 on Stadium Road.

The Inverness Courier occupied this building on Bank Street from 1838 to 2006.

Fraser Street

A view up Fraser Street, which is just off Bank Street. The Mustard Seed restaurant entrance can be seen on the left of the photograph. This is the perfect place to stop for some lunch. If you are lucky with the weather you might want to enjoy your meal on the balcony that overlooks the River Ness.

Douglas Row

At the north end of Bank Street is Douglas Row. This attractive little street with its quaint cottages is part of the riverside conservation area.

Dominican Friary

Parallel to Douglas Row is Friar's Street, where the remains of a Dominican Friary can be found in Greyfriars Cemetery (Greyfriars is a misnomer and should really be Blackfriars). The Blackfriars preached in the town and surrounding area, depending on gifts for their living. The friary was founded by Alexander II in 1233 and was a thriving community until it was disbanded during reformation in 1556. The buildings soon became ruinous, leading to stone being stolen for the construction of Cromwell's fort and the castle. Today, all that remains of the friary is a sandstone column and worn knight's effigy. The sandstone column is believed to be a section of the original choir of the monastery. The flyover that can be seen behind the column is part of a British Telecom building that sits on either side of the friary and cemetery.

The knight's effigy sits vertically on the cemetery's south wall. The effigy claims to be that of Alexander Stewart, Earl of Mar and son of Alexander Stewart, the Wolf of Badenoch.

Academy Street

Formerly known as New Street, Academy Street was renamed at the time of the old Inverness Royal Academy being built.

Inverness Royal Academy

The old Inverness Royal Academy on Academy Street was built in 1792 and was in use as a school until 1896. At this point it moved to a larger building on Midmills Road, which is now occupied by Inverness College. Prior to the formation of the Royal Academy in 1792 a Grammar School existed on Church Street at the aforementioned Dunbar Hospital. The Inverness Royal Academy moved from Midmills Road in 1977 to its present day site on Culduthel Road. The old Academy Street building is currently occupied by a clothing shop and a bar-restaurant.

Rose Street Foundry

The Rose Street Foundry has been at the heart of industrial Inverness in some form or another since 1872. This building on the corner of Academy Street and Rose Street was the Rose Street Foundry's purpose-built headquarters from 1893. The foundry was originally called 'The Northern Agricultural Implement and Foundry Company Limited' and, as well as making agricultural implements, they worked on the Highland Railway, constructed a selection of Inverness's bridges and provided ironwork for many buildings designed by the architect Alexander Ross. During World War Two, the foundry, which was now known as 'A-I Electric Welding Machines Ltd', played a vital role in the success of the D-Day landings. Welding machines supplied by the Inverness firm were used in Operation PLUTO (Pipe Line Under The Ocean). The pipeline, with over 100,000 welds, was wound around a large drum and laid underwater between Britain and France to provide a fuel supply to the Allied forces. A-I Welders are still going strong today, and can be found at Dalcross Industrial Estate on the outskirts of Inverness.

Three mosaic designs above the Rose Street Foundry second-floor windows provide a fascinating insight into the sort of duties the workmen at the foundry would have carried out.

The Cameron Monument in Station Square was erected by the 79th Queen's Own Cameron Highlanders in 1893 to honour the memory of their comrades who died in the Egypt and Sudan campaign between 1882 and 1887.

Railway Station

Inverness Railway Station opened in 1855, with it's first line linking Inverness with Nairn. Built to the designs of Joseph Mitchell, the railway quickly expanded bringing an increase in population and trade to Inverness.

A link from Nairn to Keith opened in 1858, providing a continuous line from Inverness to Aberdeen. The station was extended by Murdoch Paterson in 1876 and in 1898 the Highland Main Line was completed, connecting Inverness with Perth.

The Railway Station's main entrance can be found on Station Square, Academy Street. Station Square is also home to the Royal Highland Hotel, which can be seen on the right of this photograph. Regarded as one of Inverness's finest hotels, it was built in 1854 and known as Station Hotel until May 2000 when it was given its current name.

Six miles east of Inverness and in close proximity to Clava Cairns is the Clava or Nairn Viaduct. Rising 39 metres above the valley of the River Nairn, the viaduct is part of the Inverness–Perth rail link. At 549 metres in length and with 29 red sandstone arches, it is the longest viaduct in Scotland. It was built by Sir John Fowler and Murdoch Paterson between 1893 and 1898.

Inverness Bus Station

Just off Academy Street is Margaret Street, where Inverness Bus Station can be found.

Inverness Library

Also next to the bus station at Farraline Park is Inverness Library. It was built as a school in 1841 by William Robertson in Greek Revival style.

The school was founded by Dr Andrew Bell and known as Dr Bell's Institution or Farraline Park School. In 1937 the building ceased to be a school and in 1981 it became Inverness Public Library.

Victorian Market

The original Victorian Market was built in 1870 by the Town Council to the designs of William Lawrie and was the first covered marketplace in Inverness. Before the Victorian Market, open-air markets had been the norm in Inverness. The most notable of these was known as the Exchange, which ran the length of the High Street from Eastgate to the Town House. Pictured here is the Market Arcade.

Entry to the Market is possible from Academy Street, Union Street, Queensgate and Church Street. The Academy Street entrance, seen here, is all that survived a fire that tore through the gas-lit Market in 1889. The only life lost in the fire was that of a faithful dog who refused to leave a shop it guarded. The Victorian Market was rebuilt by Inverness Town Council in 1890–91.

Model trains run overhead at the Model Shop in the Market Hall, entertaining children and adults alike.

An impressive-looking Victorian cast-iron and wooden-domed roof can be found in the Market Hall.

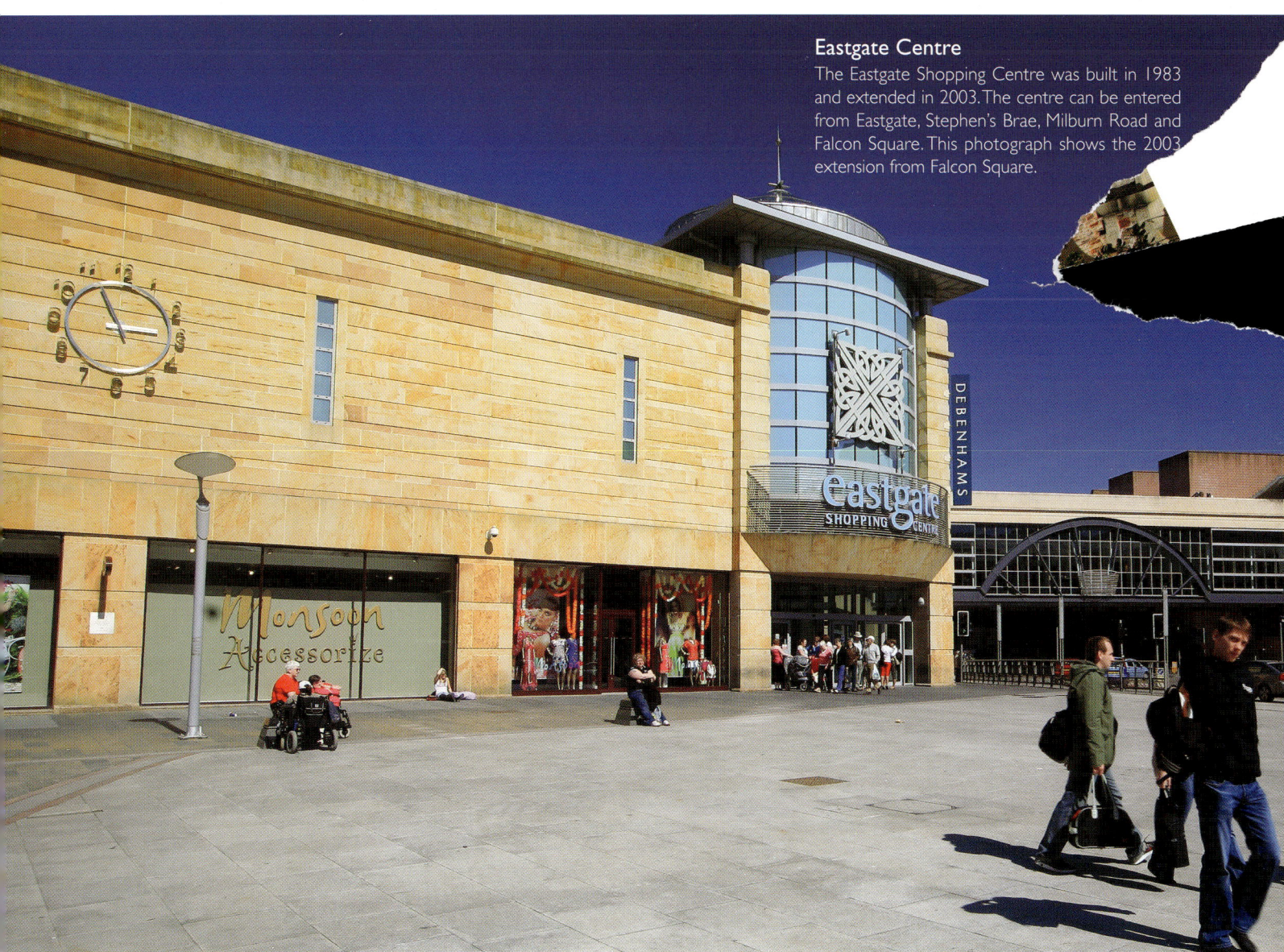

Eastgate Centre

The Eastgate Shopping Centre was built in 1983 and extended in 2003. The centre can be entered from Eastgate, Stephen's Brae, Milburn Road and Falcon Square. This photograph shows the 2003 extension from Falcon Square.

Falcon Square

The extension to the Eastgate Centre brought with it Falcon Square, which provides a space for temporary markets and an area where the city can hold outdoor gatherings. The main feature of the square is the city's new Mercat Cross, which can be seen on the right of this image. The old Mercat Cross is located in front of the Town House on Inverness High Street. Both are adorned with the Scottish unicorn.

Part of the Eastgate Centre's extension included the relocation of the listed Falconer's Building. In an ambitious operation the building was dismantled brick by brick and reconstructed 60 yards from its original position. The Category B listed building was built in 1872 to house Falcon Iron Works and Foundry, which was established by brothers John and Charlie Falconer in 1858. The old Falcon Foundry is now home to a restaurant and designer store.

Stephen's Brae

A selection of cafés with outdoor seating facilities make Stephen's Brae the perfect place to stop for a spot of lunch.

Midmills Building

Located at the top of Stephen's Brae is Midmills Building, which was purpose-built in 1895 to house the Inverness Royal Academy. The Academy stayed here until the late 1970s, when it moved to its present-day building in Culduthel Road. Midmills Building is currently home to Inverness College.

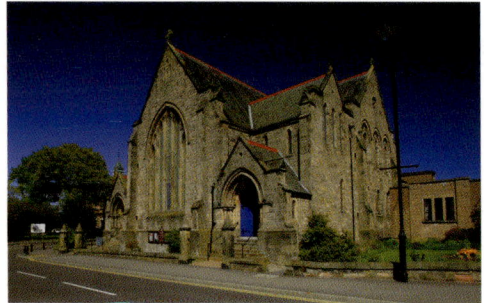

Crown Church

Across the road from Midmills Building is Crown Church, which was designed by Inverness-born architect James Robert Rhind and completed in 1901. Notably, the church was designed with a spire, but a fee of £1,000 to add it was considered too great.

Crown School

Built in 1879 and a stone's-throw from Crown Church is another fine-looking building. Crown School was home to Inverness High School after it absorbed Raining's School on Ardconnel Street in the late 19th century. In 1937 the High School moved to its present-day site on Montague Row. Today Crown School teaches children at primary level.

High Street

Inverness's bustling High Street stretches from Eastgate to Bridge Street. The High Street, which was once known as Eastgate, is pedestrian-friendly with a fine selection of small shops.

Market Brae Steps

Market Brae Steps are seen here from the High Street. In the past Inverness Meal Market was held at the bottom of the Market Brae Steps.

A view of the steps from Ardconnel Terrace. The Market Brae Steps connect Ardconnel Terrace in the Crown area of Inverness with the High Street.

Inglis Street

Inglis Street can be found at the bottom of the Market Brae Steps, where Eastgate meets the High Street. Throughout the centuries Inglis Street was one of Inverness's busiest market streets, with cattle and meal markets at either end. It was named after William Inglis, who was Provost of Inverness from 1797 to 1800.

Eastgate

A view of Eastgate from Inglis Street, which until 1900 was known as Petty Street.

Town House

Inverness Town House can be found at the point where High Street meets Bridge Street. Designed by architects Matthews and Lawrie in Victorian Gothic Style, the Town House was completed in 1882 and replaced an earlier Town House. It cost £12,500 to build, £5,000 of which was bequeathed by Duncan Grant of Bught, whose father had been Provost.

The paved area in front of the Town House, known as the Exchange, was the site of weekly markets which sold local country produce. It was also the spot from which important town announcements, such as fairs, would be made.

Mercat Cross

The Mercat Cross stood in the middle of Inverness High Street until 1768 when it moved to this spot in front of the Town House. It replaced an earlier Mercat Cross which had been destroyed in the late 16th century during a clan raid. By law local goods had to be sold in the town so a tax could be levied on each item. An officer would survey these goods at the Mercat Cross before they could be put up for sale on the High Street. In 1882 the Cross was moved to Castle Wynd and in 1900 it was restored and returned to its present location by Robert Finlay, who was the Attorney General for England and Wales and later became Lord Chancellor. He added the Scottish unicorn and town's arms to the Mercat Cross and had the Clach na Cùdainn embedded into its base.

Clach na Cùdainn (Stone)

Clach na Cùdainn roughly means 'stone of the tubs'. It was where women would stop for a breather and lay their baskets down after doing their washing down at the river. Before the Clach na Cùdainn joined the Mercat Cross it sat opposite Castle Wynd at the top of Bridge Street. The stone was very popular with emigrants, who chipped chunks off it to take with them as lucky charms. This led to the stone being sunk into the base of the Mercat Cross and covered in asphalt.

Castle Street

The name Castle Street (it is seen here from the north end) did not come into use until 1675. The street is one of Inverness's oldest and had previously been known as Overgait and Doomsdale. Excavation work, carried out in 1979, found evidence that the lower part of Castle Street may have been inhabited as early as 7000 BC.

Floral Clock

Inverness's Floral Clock can be found halfway up Castle Street on Castle Mound. The clock, like many throughout Scotland, was inspired by Edinburgh's equivalent, which was created by John McHattie in 1903.

The Floral Clock incorporates the names of Inverness's three sister towns/cities in its design. The first city to be twinned with Inverness was Augsburg in 1956. The idea came from the Government, who wanted to promote friendly links between Germany and Britain in the aftermath of World War Two. In 1981, La Baule in France became the second town to be twinned with Inverness. This evolved through a connection between councillors from the two towns. The most recent town to be twinned with Inverness is St Valery-en-Caux in 1987. Links with the French town date back to 1940 when the 51st Highland Division were captured there by the German military. The locals were said to have been very welcoming to the troops and in 1944 their kindness was repaid when the Division returned to liberate the town.

Castle Street shops

On Castle Street you will find J. Graham & Co., which sells outdoor equipment. Established in 1857, Graham's also sell fishing permits for the River Ness and hire out boats at Loch Ruthven. Next door to Graham's is a local institution, the Castle Restaurant, where you will find good honest food and a friendly service. A little further up Castle Street is the well-established kilt and tartan specialists, Chisholm's Highland Dress.

Ardkeen Tower

Up the hill from Castle Street, on Culduthel Road, is Ardkeen Tower, which sits on a mound known as 'Hill of the Heads'. It is believed the mound gained its unsavoury nickname due to it being the site of town beheadings and hangings.

In 1834 Ardkeen Tower was built as the Inverness United Charities Institution, which housed a juvenile female school. The building, which has also been used as an observatory, is now privately owned.

Inverness Baptist Church

Inverness Baptist Church was founded in 1898 and held its first services on School Lane. In 1901 the church built what was intended to be a temporary place of worship on Friars Lane. It was constructed from corrugated iron and known locally as the 'tin Kirk'. In 1933, Inverness Baptist Church moved to this building on Castle Street.

View Place
Looking up View Place (right) and down Castle Road.

Ness Bank

Just off Castle Road is Ness Bank. Here you will find plenty of restaurants, all with lovely views of the River Ness. Ness Bank is seen here from the Infirmary Bridge.

Ness Bank Church

Ness Bank is home to Ness Bank Church, which was built in 1901 by William Mackintosh in Early Gothic Revival Style.

This view of Ness Bank Church is from Inverness Castle.

Ness Bank Church Gardens

Next to Ness Bank Church are the beautifully kept Ness Bank Gardens.

Cavell Gardens

A walk along Ness Bank leads to Cavell Gardens. The gardens are named after nurse Edith Cavell, who was born in Norfolk in 1865. Cavell was executed in 1915 for helping Allied soldiers escape German-occupied Brussels during World War One.

In 1922 this monument was erected in Cavell Gardens in memory of the men who laid down their lives during World War One.

This Lime Tree in Cavell Gardens was planted in 1911 to commemorate the coronation of King George V, by Mrs Birnie, wife of Provost John Birnie.

Ladies Walk

From Cavell Gardens it is possible to continue walking along the riverside via Ladies Walk.

Forbes Fountain

Forbes Fountain can be found at the end of Ladies Walk. Forbes Fountain originally sat in front of the Town House and protected the Clach na Cùdainn (stone of the tubs). The fountain, which once had a canopy, was presented to the town in 1880 by Dr G.F. Forbes.

Ness Walk

Crossing the Infirmary Bridge at Cavell Gardens leads to Ness Walk on the west side of the River Ness.

Royal Northern Infirmary
The Royal Northern Infirmary on Ness Walk was built in 1803 and is used today as a community hospital. In 1896 this chapel was added to the Royal Northern Infirmary.

Raigmore Hospital
Raigmore Hospital on Old Perth Road was established in 1941. A series of new buildings were opened at Raigmore in 1970 and with continued growth over the years it has become Inverness's main hospital.

Hilton Hospital

Located on Old Edinburgh Road (also known as General Wade's Military Road), Inverness Poorhouse was built between 1859 and 1861. Designed by James Matthews and William Lawrie, Inverness Poor House came to be known as the Muirfield Institution before settling on the title of Hilton Hospital. The building has now been converted into flats.

A view from Ness Walk of the River Ness and Inverness Castle.

The Cathedral

Just off Ness Walk, on the corner of Bishop's Road and Ardross Street, is Inverness Cathedral, which was designed by Alexander Ross and built between 1866 and 1869.

The cathedral's towers were originally designed to have spires. Due to a lack of funding, they were never added.

Inverness Cathedral's choir stalls were built using Austrian oak in 1909.

A close-up of the cathedral's beautiful west window. As one of the largest stained-glass windows in Scotland, it depicts the Last Judgement.

The main entrance to the cathedral is framed by some impressive-looking carvings. Above the door is a carving by Thomas Earp of Christ's Missionary Commission to the Apostles. The statues on either side of the doorway are of Saints Andrew, Peter, Paul and John the Baptist.

A view of Huntly Street and the River Ness from Douglas Row.

Huntly Street
At the end of Ness Walk continue along the riverside onto Huntly Street.

Kiltmaker
For anyone interested in the history and culture of Scotland's national dress, the Scottish Kiltmaker Visitor Centre on Huntly Street is well worth a visit.

The Kitchen
Also on Huntly Street is the Kitchen, where you can expect an excellent meal with superb views of the River Ness and Inverness Castle.

St Mary's Church

St Mary's Church on Huntly Street was the first Catholic church to be built in Inverness after the Reformation. Designed by William Robertson, it was completed in 1837 in Perpendicular Gothic Style.

Cromwell's Tower

In the unlikely surroundings of the Longman industrial estate stands a rather elegant-looking Clock Tower. This is known as Cromwell's Tower and is pretty much all that remains of Oliver Cromwell's citadel.

The citadel, which was built in order to subdue the Highlands, was a five-sided fortification made up of large earthy mounds (seen here) and stone that was acquired from local buildings. Stone from Greyfriars Church and the monasteries of Beauly and Kinloss aided its construction, along with timber from Strathglass and oak transported from England. Described as a strong fortification, the citadel was one of many built in Scotland by Cromwell's army and is believed to have cost £80,000. Built from the period 1652 to 1658, it was capable of accommodating 1,000 men, many of whom, it is said, went on to settle in Inverness. 1661 saw the citadel dismantled at the request of the Highland chiefs following the Restoration of Charles II in 1660.

Balnain House

Balnain House was built in 1726 and was lived in until the 1960s when it fell into disrepair. It was used as a hospital for Government troops immediately after the Battle of Culloden in 1746. In 1993, the building was restored by the National Trust for Scotland. It then became the Home of Highland Music until it closed at the end of the 20th century. Balnain House is now the regional office of the National Trust for Scotland.

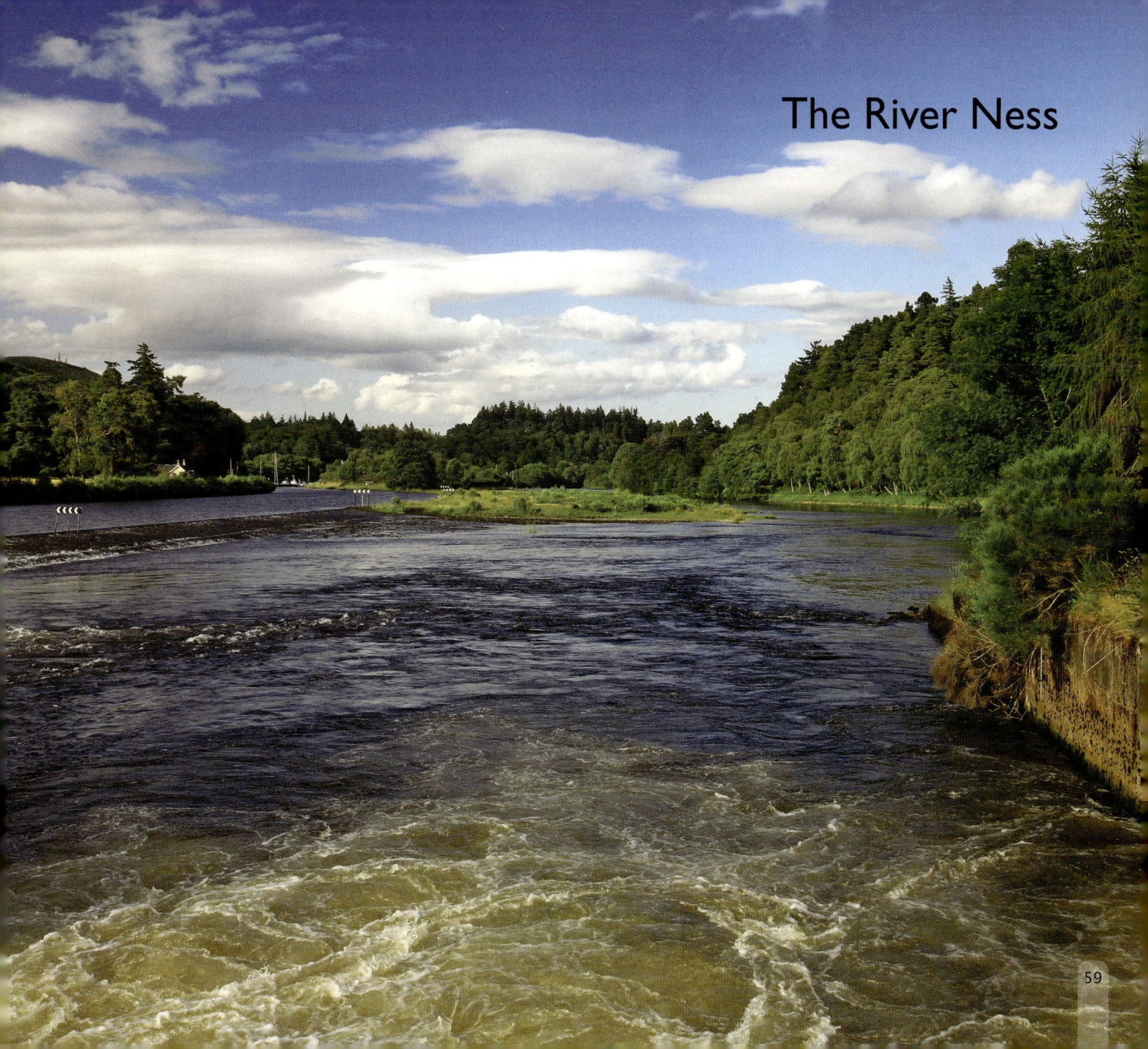

The River Ness

The River Ness begins its six-mile journey at the northern end of Loch Dochfour. It then flows north along the Great Glen, passing through the centre of Inverness on its way to the Beauly Firth. The River Ness is seen here at its starting point. On the left of the image is the Caledonian Canal, which is separated from the River Ness by Dochgarroch Weir.

The River Ness has many tributaries, including Holm Burn, which is seen here at Torbreck Falls.

The banks of the Ness look particularly beautiful in autumn.

Looking upstream towards Inverness Castle from Friar's Bridge.

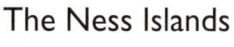

Evening sunshine through foliage in the islands.

The Ness Islands

The Ness Islands are a natural beauty spot that can found less than a mile upstream from the city centre. The Islands are connected by a series of bridges that create the most enjoyable method of crossing the River Ness. Before Joseph Mitchell built the first bridges in the 19th century the Ness Islands were only accessible by boat. As a Civil Engineer, Joseph Mitchell helped raise funds to have bridges built and supervised their construction. Today the Ness Islands attract a great deal of tourists and provide a beautiful recreational area for the people of Inverness.

Joseph Mitchell's first bridge stood at the Island Bank Road entrance to the Ness Islands. It has since been the site of several bridges, including the present-day suspension bridge we see here.

The Islands really come to life during the autumn months.

This suspension bridge connects the islands (right) with the Bught area of the city.

Nessie ventures onto dry land!

The main focal point of the islands is a seated area where a mixture of impressive stone, wood and metal work can be found.

Infirmary Bridge

The Infirmary Bridge is the smaller of the two main suspension footbridges that cross the River Ness. It will rock and sway, almost alarmingly, with a couple of people or more crossing it. Children in particular enjoy bouncing along the bridge to increase its swaying motion.

Built in 1879 by W. Smith and Son at Ness Iron Works, the bridge crosses the river between Cavell Gardens and the Royal Northern Infirmary.

A view of the Ness Bridge from Inverness Castle with the Greig Street Bridge and Friar's Bridge further downstream.

Ness Bridge

Since the 11th century there has been a Ness Bridge in some form or another. The early bridges were insubstantial timber structures that would succumb to the force of the River Ness fairly swiftly. The last of these was said by an officer of Cromwell to be 'the weakest that ever straddled over so strong a stream'. This bridge collapsed in 1664 and a seven-arch stone bridge was built in its place, which lasted until 1849 when it was swept away by floods. Six years later, and in an effort to prevent bridge pylons being washed away by flooding, a suspension bridge was completed. It was an attractive bridge with a stone archway on its east side giving it plenty of character. Sadly, it was deconstructed in 1959 as it could no longer cope with the increasing volume of traffic crossing the Ness. A temporary bridge was put in place marginally upstream until the present-day Ness Bridge (seen here from Huntly Street) was completed in 1961.

The Ness Bridge features colourful floodlighting at night.

Greig Street Bridge

The Greig Street Bridge is a suspension footbridge that was built in 1881 by the Rose Street Foundry to carry its employees across the River Ness. It is Inverness's most iconic and photographed bridge and, like its little brother the Infirmary Bridge, it too undulates under the weight of more than one or two bodies. The Greig Street Bridge is, however, both larger and sturdier and therefore not quite so unnerving.

Friar's Bridge

Friars Bridge was built in 1987 to relieve congestion in the town centre. This pre-stressed concrete arch bridge is now the main road crossing in Inverness, carrying local and A82 traffic away from the city centre.

Waterloo Bridge (Black Bridge)

The Waterloo Bridge was completed in 1896 by the Rose Street Foundry to replace the original wooden structure. Designed by John A. Mackenzie and Murdoch Paterson, the bridge comprises steel trusses mounted on iron piers. The aforementioned wooden bridge was built in 1808 and, due to the dark wood used in its construction, it became known locally as the Black Bridge. The present bridge has hung onto this nickname.

Ness Viaduct

The Ness Viaduct is a steel-beam railway bridge that was built in 1989 after the original five-arch masonry bridge was swept away by flooding. It was swiftly constructed after the collapse due to its importance as a rail link to the north. The original bridge was built in 1862 by the runner-up in a competition to build the Ness Bridge.

Inverness Harbour

Further downstream is Inverness Harbour, which is one of Scotland's most sheltered natural deep water harbours. The harbour, seen here from Shore Street, dates back to 1249.

In 2008 Inverness Harbour was extended to the mouth of the River Ness creating the 150-berth Inverness Marina.

The Beauly Firth signals the end of the River Ness's six-mile journey northwards from Loch Dochfour.

The Common Seal can be found in the Moray Firth, Beauly Firth and River Ness. They will swim up the River Ness chasing salmon and trout, making it possible to see them in the city centre. This Common Seal pup was photographed near Inverness on the shores of the Beauly Firth.

Kessock Bridge

The Kessock Bridge is a cable-stayed bridge that carries the A9 trunk road across the Beauly Firth.

Prior to the existence of the Kessock Bridge motorists had the choice of either heading inland round the Beauly Firth or using the Kessock Ferry. The Kessock Ferryboat crossed the Beauly Firth between North and South Kessock until the completion of the Kessock Bridge in 1982.

The Highland Year of Culture 2007 comes to an end with a fireworks display at the Kessock Bridge.

The Kessock Bridge rises high above sea level to provide plenty of clearance for ships navigating the Beauly Firth, Inverness Harbour and Caledonian Canal.

Inverness Castle

The south block of Inverness Castle (seen here) was built by architect William Burn between 1833 and 1836. The statue in front of the castle is that of Jacobite heroine Flora MacDonald.

Castle Hill has been the site of a number of fortifications since the 12th century. During times of conflict Inverness Castle was destroyed and rebuilt several times. It was razed to the ground for the last time in 1746 when Bonnie Prince Charlie ordered its demolition during the second major Jacobite uprising. It then lay in ruins until work began on the present-day castle in 1833.

The octagonal and rounded towers of the north block, seen here from Bridge Street, were designed to complement the south block's circular tower.

The setting sun casts the Flora MacDonald statue into silhouette. Flora MacDonald earned her place in history by helping Bonnie Prince Charlie escape Government troops after the Battle of Culloden by disguising the Prince as Irish maid Betty Burke.

Less than a mile north-east of Inverness Castle is Auldcastle Road in the residential area of Crown. An archaeological dig found evidence that a castle may have existed on this site around the 11th century. A two metre-thick dressed stone wall was uncovered along with fish bones and a silver coin dating back to the 12th century. Fire damage to the dressed stone wall may provide evidence to support the theory that the castle was held by King Macbeth. It is said that Malcolm Canmore burned down the castle in 1056 as revenge for the death of his father King Duncan at the hands of Macbeth in 1040.

The grounds of Inverness Castle are home to an abundance of rabbits.

Around half a mile south-east of Auldcastle Road on Old Perth Road is King Duncan's Well and Grave. King Duncan I was king of Scotland from 1034 until 1040 when he was killed by Macbeth at a battle just outside Elgin. His body would have traditionally been taken to royal burial grounds on the island of Iona, making it unlikely that the well on Old Perth Road is his final resting place.

Battle of Culloden

On 16 April 1746 the last major battle to be fought on British soil took place five miles east of Inverness at what is now known as Culloden Moor. It is probably best to first cover the many years of conflict that led to this battle. The Battle of Culloden was in fact the last chapter of a sporadic civil war that started in 1688. King James VII of Scotland and II of England was a Roman Catholic who believed in the Divine Right of Kings (a doctrine stating that a monarch is subject to no earthly authority). Because of this he became unpopular and in 1688 Parliament invited William of Orange and his wife Mary (James VII/II's daughter by his first wife, a Protestant) to rule. In 1689 James was deposed, giving William and Mary joint rulership. This led to the start of the Jacobite Rebellion. The word Jacobite comes from the Latin for James, which is Jacobus, hence the Jacobite Rebellion, which would see three major attempts at restoring James and his descendants to the throne.

Charles Edward Stuart, known as the Young Pretender or Bonnie Prince Charlie, led the Jacobite Rebellion of 1745. He was the son of James Francis Edward Stuart (the Old Pretender) who had arrived in Scotland for the 1715 Rebellion only to quickly return to France when unable to inspire a disheartened army to fight for him. Charles, who was the grandson of the overthrown King James VII/II, arrived at Eriskay on 23 July 1745 looking to raise an army, but there was to be no immediate response. This led Charles to raise his father's standard at Glenfinnan on the Scottish mainland, where he managed to gather a large enough force of Highland clansmen to march on the city of Edinburgh. The capital quickly surrendered and on 21 September 1745 Charles defeated the only Government army in Scotland at the Battle of Prestonpans. By November 1745 Charles had built an army 6,000 strong which marched south, taking Carlisle on its way to Derby, where there would be a make-or-break decision to be made. The Prince was not getting the English Jacobite support that he had expected, so he reluctantly returned to Scotland with his army. On 18 February 1746 the Jacobite army arrived in Inverness and found the town evacuated. A garrison, however, had been left at the castle. Two days later Inverness Castle was blown up by the Prince and from then until the Battle of Culloden Inverness was regarded as his headquarters.

The Government soldiers were led by the Duke of Cumberland, who had obtained large numbers of reinforcements from the Continent. On the retreat of the Jacobites from Stirling at the beginning of February, the Duke of Cumberland had followed them as far as Perth. He then marched to Aberdeen where he stayed for a time. On 8 April he left Aberdeen with a well-organised army that was supported by sea-vessels in the Moray Firth. He reached Nairn on Monday 14 April. The 15 April was the Duke's 25th birthday and the date of a failed night attack by the Jacobites. At eight o'clock on the evening of the 15th Charles's men marched towards Nairn, but in the darkness progress was slow and within four miles of Nairn day began to break. The Jacobites had also received word that the sound of a drum could be heard at the Duke's camp, which meant the Government soldiers were on alert. The men returned hungry and dispirited to Culloden Moor, where they arrived at around eight in the morning.

At eight o'clock Jacobite pickets made their first sighting of the Government's advance guard. Cumberland's informers let him know that the enemy was situated at Culloden Moor, about two miles from Culloden House. By 11 o'clock the armies were only two miles apart, with Cumberland advancing, and just before one o'clock both sides were in position. The 5,000 hungry and exhausted Jacobite soldiers stood about 400–500 yards from the 9,000 well-rested Government soldiers. It is very much worth noting that this was not simply a battle between the English and the Scots. The bulk of the Jacobite army was made up of Highlanders and reinforced with French and Irish soldiers. Three of the Government's infantry battalions were Scottish units. This created an unbearable situation where families were split as brothers fought brothers and fathers fought sons.

At one o'clock on 16 April 1746 the Jacobite artillery opened fire on the Duke's men, and they duly responded with their own artillery strike. The Jacobites were bombarded by the government's superior artillery and were waiting for the order to charge. They eventually charged through hail of cannon-fire, smoke, gunfire and grapeshot. Unfortunately for the Jacobites, the Government troops had at last found a way to challenge the notoriously effective Highland charge. The Jacobites lost all shape and confidence and at this point started to flee. It had taken less than an hour for the Duke of Cumberland's men to defeat the Jacobites and, although the battle was relatively short, it was extremely bloody.

It is said that Charles stayed at the battle for as long as any hope lingered and, when his men were retreating, he proposed leading them on foot to the charge. His officers would not allow this and so he reluctantly retreated. He roamed the Highlands for the next few months and, with a £30,000 reward for his capture, his followers showed incredible loyalty in protecting him. The Prince escaped as far as the island of Benbecula, where he met Flora MacDonald, who would be instrumental in plotting his escape. On 27 June 1746 Charles and Flora sailed from Benbecula to Skye with the Prince disguised as Flora's maid, Betty Burke. They then travelled by foot to Portree, on the way avoiding Government troops. At this point they parted company, never to meet again, and the Prince was able to obtain passage to France and successfully escape.

For Inverness and the Highlands the aftermath of the Battle of Culloden was difficult, to say the least. Immediately after the battle the Duke of Cumberland marched to Inverness, where he raided homes looking for Jacobites. It is said that all were swiftly put to the end of a musket, bayonet or hangman's rope, or burnt alive in their homes. Women, children, old and young were all included, the orders were 'No Quarter Given' and none was. Over the coming months the Hanoverian assault on Jacobite sympathisers continued with the breakdown of the clan system and the banning of the kilt and tartan. The bagpipes were made illegal and any utterance of the Gaelic language was also prohibited. Barracks and roads were built to better control the region, with Government forces stationed throughout the Highlands. A new fortress called Fort George was built to the east of Inverness and the only wearing of the kilt sanctioned was in the Highland regiments that served the British Army.

Flora MacDonald looking west from Inverness Castle.

A view over the battlefield from the roof of the new visitor centre, which opened in 2007.

This Memorial Cairn stands some 20ft high and was erected by Duncan Forbes in 1881.

The Clan Cameron Stone. There are many stones marking the graves of the clans to be found throughout the battlefield, though no one really knows who was buried where by the folk of Inverness who came out to bury the fallen.

Contrary to the inscription, there is no record of where the fallen Government troops were buried. 'Field of the English' isn't entirely accurate either, as the Government forces were made up of three Scottish infantry regiments.

This stone marks the spot where Alexander MacGillivray, commander of the Clan Chattan, fell.

THE BATTLE OF CULLODEN WAS FOUGHT ON THIS MOOR 16TH APRIL 1746. THE GRAVES OF THE GALLANT HIGHLANDERS WHO FOUGHT FOR SCOTLAND & PRINCE CHARLIE ARE MARKED BY THE NAMES OF THEIR CLANS.

The Memorial Cairn includes this inscription.

This heather-thatched cottage, known as the farmhouse of Leanach, survived the battle and has been restored numerous times.

Blue flags mark the Jacobite front line.

While red flags mark the Government front line.

Culloden House

Culloden House is now a luxury hotel which stands in nearly 40 acres of beautiful parkland. The hotel dates back to the 16th century, although it was redesigned and rebuilt between 1772 and 1788, becoming the Georgian mansion we see today.

Culloden House is famed for having been the lodgings of Bonnie Prince Charlie and his chief officers prior to the Battle of Culloden.

Fort George

Fort George can be found around 15 miles east of Inverness on a spit of land that juts out into the Moray Firth. It is named after George II, who ordered that it be built following the Battle of Culloden as a solution to the threat posed by the Jacobites. Fort George is considered to be one of the most impressive fortifications in Europe. It was designed by Lieutenant-General William Skinner and took 21 years (1748–69) to complete, by which time the Highlands were peaceful. The western walls of Fort George are seen here from Chanonry Point on the opposite side of the Moray Firth.

This bridge, which leads to the Principal Gate, was built in 1766.

At the end of the bridge is the Principal Gate itself, which was completed in 1756. Above the gate is King George II's coat of arms. The Scottish segment of the arms is incorrect – it should include a double border around the insignia.

The soldiers' guardrooms can be found after passing through the Principal Gate.

Looking back on the Principal Gate from the Parade inside Fort George.

The garrison buildings were built between 1753 and 1767. From left to right are the Governor's House, the Artillery Block, the Staff Block and the Regimental Museum. With Fort George still used as an army base today, the majority of the garrison buildings are closed to the public. The grassed area in the foreground is known as the Parade and is used for events such as ceremonial parades.

Fort George's ramparts are around a kilometre long and are equipped with over 70 guns, which have yet to fire a single shot in anger.

The chapel interior.

Fort George Chapel, seen here from the south, is thought to have been designed by Robert Adam. The chapel is still used as a place of worship by soldiers stationed at Fort George today.

With safety in mind the Grand Magazine was built in one of the bastions with a tall blast wall to keep it separate from the rest of Fort George. It was also designed to withstand a direct hit from the strongest armament at the time, a 13-inch mortar bomb.

It is now home to the Seafield Collection, which is an impressive selection of late 18th-century arms and military equipment.

One of several stained-glass windows to be found in the chapel.

Fort George is 42 acres in size and cost more than £200,000 to build, which is about £20 million in today's money.

Caledonian Canal

The aftermath of the Battle of Culloden brought about a mass exodus of the Jacobite clans in the Highlands. By the start of the 19th century the Government was becoming increasingly worried by this trend, so in an effort to reduce the migration they began commissioning public works in the Highlands. The largest of these can be found in the stunningly beautiful Great Glen. The Caledonian Canal is a man-made waterway which connects the west coast with the east coast of Scotland. From Corpach to Inverness there are 29 locks and 10 bridges that make up the canal. It was designed by engineer Thomas Telford and took 19 years to complete, finally opening in 1822. By this time it was 12 years over schedule and had cost the British Government over £900,000 – nearly double what had been estimated. Unfortunately, due to its lack of depth the canal was never a great commercial success, meaning most vessels would continue to take the longer route around the north coast of Scotland. That being said, the Caledonian Canal is an extraordinary feat of engineering and in more recent times it has been given a new lease of life with the popularity of leisure craft. Maintained and run by British Waterways, the canal is 60 miles in length, 22 of those miles man-made, with the rest formed naturally by Loch Dochfour, Loch Ness, Loch Oich, and Loch Lochy.

Somebody's pride and joy receives maintenance at Corpach with the UK's highest mountain, Ben Nevis, in the background.

The 60-mile journey along the Great Glen is just starting for this fishing vessel waiting to enter Corpach Sea Lock from Loch Linnhe.

Not far from Corpach at Banavie is Neptune's Staircase, which is the largest of the three staircase flights to be found along the Caledonian Canal.

The view towards Loch Linnhe from the summit of Neptune's Staircase.

Neptune's Staircase climbs 64ft through eight locks. To rise through the staircase the first gate opens to allow a boat to pass through. The first gate then closes, leaving the boat in the first lock. The second gate then opens sluice hatches, which allow water to flow into the first lock and balance the level between the first and second lock. The second gate then opens to allow the boat to pass through. This gate then closes and the process is repeated until the boat has passed through all the locks. The locks on the Caledonian Canal are 40ft wide and all but one are between 170ft and 180ft long.

The view from the swing bridge at Fort Augustus.

Having negotiated the five locks at Fort Augustus this pleasure craft heads through the last gate and the open swing bridge on its way to Loch Ness.

From Banavie to Gairlochy and Loch Lochy the canal twists through some glorious landscape.

Looking north from Tomnahurich, where the towpaths make for a lovely walk along the canal banks.

The award-winning *Jacobite Cruiser*, seen here at Tomnahurich, is a superb way to experience the beauty of the Caledonian Canal and Loch Ness. One of the many delights of this cruise includes a unique look at the ruins of Urquhart Castle.

The bridge keeper opens Tomnahurich Swing Bridge allowing this small pleasure cruiser to pass through.

The Muirtown flight in Inverness is the last set of locks to be manoeuvred before Clachnaharry Sea Lock.

As part of Scottish Homecoming Year 2009 (a celebration inviting expatriates to visit their homeland) an Aviat Husky amphibious seaplane lands in Muitown Basin.

'The Gutty Slippers' add a contemporary twist to the bagpipes and in the process keep the crowd well entertained during the Muirtown Basin celebrations.

Clachnaharry Sea Lock opens up onto the Beauly Firth, ending our journey along the magnificent Caledonian Canal.

The sun sets on the Beauly Firth.

The world-famous Loch Ness can be found around eight miles south-west of Inverness. Loch Ness is roughly 23 miles long (37km) and holds a greater volume of water than all the lakes and rivers of England and Wales combined. At certain points the loch is over a mile wide and plunges to depths of over 750ft (230m).

Loch Ness makes up a major portion of the Great Glen, which is a geological fault line running from Fort William to Inverness. The Great Glen can be walked via a path known as the Great Glen Way. This image of Loch Ness was captured from Meall Fuar-Mhonaidh, a 2,293ft (699m) mountain near Drumnadrochit.

Meall Fuar-Mhonaidh, seen here from the south side of Loch Ness, is also known as the pudding bowl due to its rounded shape.

Loch Ness is one of four lochs that help make up the Caledonian Canal. The others are Loch Lochy, Loch Oich and Loch Dochfour.

Loch Ness is of course universally known for its mysterious monster. The earliest recorded sighting of the Loch Ness monster occurred notably at the River Ness, not Loch Ness, in AD 565 when St Columba was on his way to meet with King Brude. Columba came across a group of Picts burying a man beside the River Ness. The Picts explained that the man had been swimming across the river when a large 'water beast' attacked him and dragged him under. They said they had tried to pull him from the river but were only able to drag up his corpse. Columba then stunned the Picts by telling one of his followers to swim across the river. His devoted follower began swimming the river and the beast came after him. It is said that St Columba then made the sign of the cross and commanded the monster to 'Go no further. Do not touch the man. Go back at once.' The beast is understood to have instantly stopped, as if it had been 'pulled back with ropes' and fled in terror, and both Columba's men and the pagan Picts praised God for the miracle.

Modern interest in the Loch Ness monster began in 1933 when George Spicer and his wife claimed to have seen a large creature cross the road in front of their car. The following year a well-respected British surgeon by the name of Robert Wilson photographed what was believed to be the proof that the Loch Ness monster existed. The image, which is known as the 'Surgeon's Photo', turned out to be a fake. A toy submarine and model sea serpent were used to stage the hoax. Since then many photographs claiming to be of the monster have been captured as 'Nessie hunters' continue to be drawn to Loch Ness in search of the elusive Loch Ness monster.

A view from Fort Augustus of the southern end of Loch Ness.

Aldourie Castle

At the north-eastern end of Loch Ness, not far from Dores, sits the elegant looking Aldourie Castle, which dates back to the 17th century.

Boleskine House

On the south-eastern shores of Loch Ness lies a house shrouded in mystery. Boleskine House was built in the late 18th century as a hunting lodge for noble gentlemen. It gained notoriety when it was bought by controversial occultist Aleister Crowley, who lived at the house from 1899 to 1913. The building was made famous when Led Zeppelin guitarist and reputed Crowley enthusiast Jimmy Page bought Boleskine House in the 1970s.

Across the road from Boleskine House is Boleskine Graveyard, which can be seen here with Loch Ness in the background.

Foyers Falls

Around two miles south of Boleskine House is the village of Foyers, where a forest walk which leads to Foyers Falls can be found. Pine martens, red squirrels and deer are among the wildlife that have made Foyers Woods their home.

One of Foyers Falls' most famous visitors was Scotland's national poet Robert Burns. On seeing the falls he is said to have immediately taken out his pencil and written a verse. His words are engraved on stones, which can be seen dotted along the forest path to the Falls.

Water from Foyers Falls rushes through underground tunnels on its way to turbines that create hydro-electricity.

Urquhart Castle's defensive ditch is crossed via a stone causeway and bridge.

Urquhart Castle

The ruins of Urquhart Castle lie about 16 miles south-west of Inverness on the north-western banks of Loch Ness. Urquhart Castle was built on a rocky promontory that is thought to have been used as a place of defence since Pictish times. The castle itself dates back to the 13th century when it was considered a major fortress. Over the next 500 years it was attacked and rebuilt many times until it was finally left in the ruinous state that we see today.

The ditch is on average five metres deep and 30 metres across at its widest point. The modern fixed bridge which can be seen here was once the location of the castle's drawbridge. The upper levels of the gatehouse can be seen lying on the grass. After the Jacobite Rebellion of 1689–90 the Grant Highlanders who had been garrisoned at the castle reportedly destroyed parts of the fortress (including the gatehouse) so as to prevent it from becoming a future Jacobite stronghold.

Urquhart Castle provides Nessie hunters with excellent views over Loch Ness. In the foreground is the dovecot which was where the pigeons would have been kept. Dovecots were a common feature of mediaeval castles, providing a regular supply of meat and eggs.

The view from the visitor centre café at Urquhart Castle. The visitor centre features an excellent audio-visual presentation which is well worth seeing.

Between Urquhart Castle and its visitor centre is a life-size replica of a trebuchet, which was used for firing stone balls at the walls of castles during mediaeval times.

Urquhart Castle and Loch Ness from the top of Grant Tower.

Parks and Leisure

Whin Park

Whin Park is a children's play park, which can be found around a mile or so upstream from Inverness city centre. Situated on the northern banks of the River Ness, Whin Park is one of several parks that surround the Ness Islands.

The highlight at Whin Park is the Ness Islands Railway, which is a fully operational miniature railway.

Children will love Whin Park's adventure playground, which includes chutes, swings, see-saws and climbing frames.

Whin Park boating pond from the boatman's hut. The building in the background is now a shop but was once used in conjunction with a lade to provide hydro-electricity.

The miniature railway crosses this bridge which was once used as a foot bridge in the Ness Islands.

The Aircrew Memorial Bandstand is dedicated to those who flew from the north of Scotland during World War Two and did not return. The bandstand holds free concerts on most Sunday afternoons throughout the summer.

Bellfield Park's tennis courts were opened in 1953.

Bellfield Park

Bellfield Park can be found directly across from the Ness Islands on Island Bank Road. It is a family-orientated park with gardens, a children's play area, a paddling pool, tennis courts, a putting green, a bandstand and even an outdoor gym.

Bught Park

Situated next to the Ness Islands on the western banks of the River Ness is Inverness's largest park. Bught Park is made up of shinty and football pitches and is host to large events such as the Inverness Highland Games.

Shinty

Shinty is an ancient Scottish game involving two teams of 12 players striking a leather ball using curved sticks known as camans. Shinty is played on a grass pitch with goals at either end. The aim of the game is to score more goals than your opponent. This image shows Newtonmore and Kingussie contesting the 2009 MacTavish Cup Final at Bught Park.

A view from Bught Park Stadium, where Inverness Shinty Club play all their home games.

Newtonmore celebrate winning the 2009 MacTavish Cup Final after beating Kingussie by five goals to four in a thoroughly entertaining game.

Inverness British Legion Pipe Band perform at the 2009 Highland Games.

Highland Games

The Inverness Highland Games is an annual event which takes place at Bught Park. The games consist of Highland dancing, track events, piping, traditional music and heavy events such as tossing the caber. The Inverness Highland Games are just one of many Highland Games that take place throughout Scotland. Although the date of the very first Inverness Games is unknown, in 1822 *The Inverness Courier* reported that fundraising was taking place to revive the gathering. Since then the Inverness Highland Games has firmly established itself as one of the finest games in the north of Scotland.

The spectators' favourite, the caber toss involves running while balancing a long tapered wooden pole and tossing it so that the top end of the caber hits the ground first. The caber should land with the top end facing the thrower and the bottom end pointing exactly away from the thrower. Competitors are judged on how straight their caber lands. A good throw would see the caber sitting in the 12 o'clock position, relative to the thrower's run.

Fireworks
The annual bonfire and fireworks display in Inverness draws thousands of spectators to Bught Park.

Sports Centre

Two minutes walk from Bught Park is Inverness Sports Centre, where the facilities are excellent.

The running track next to the Sports Centre is known as Queens Park Athletics Stadium. It is the home of Inverness Harriers Athletics Club and the finishing point for numerous local races, including the Loch Ness Marathon.

Inverness Aquadome comprises a leisure pool, flumes, a thistle-shaped outdoor pool and a 25-metre competition pool.

Northern Meeting Park

Next to Inverness Cathedral is Northern Meeting Park, where Northern Counties Cricket Club play their home matches. The park, which features a 19th-century grandstand, also holds city events such as the Inverness Tattoo.

Inverness Golf Course

Inverness Golf Course is one of three golf courses in Inverness. It was established in the 1880s and can be found on Culcabock Road.

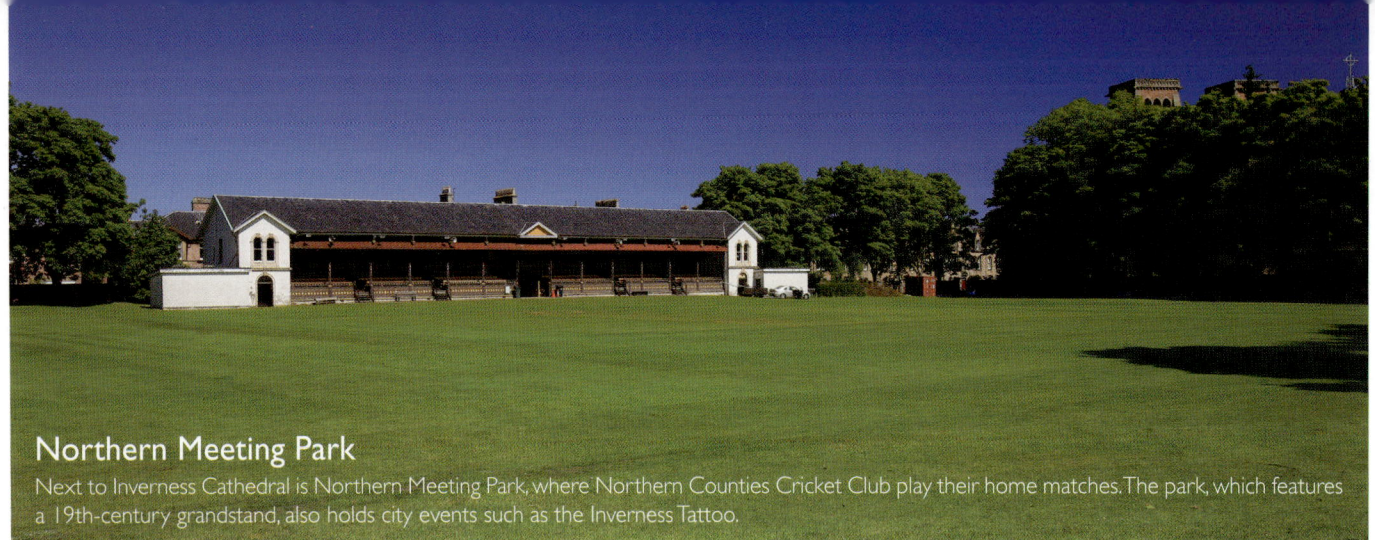

Torvean Golf Course

Torvean Golf Course was opened in 1961 and is located in the south-west of Inverness, next to the Caledonian Canal.

Fairways

Fairways opened in 1989 and comprises a 19-bay driving range, a restaurant, a bar, a golf shop and Inverness's newest 18-hole golf course.

Eden Court

Eden Court Theatre is the largest arts and entertainment venue in the Highlands. It can be found on the riverside next to Inverness Cathedral and was built in 1976 after the closure of the Empire Theatre on Academy Street – which had been Inverness's only theatre.

Bishop's Palace, which sits alongside Eden Court, was built in 1878 by members of the Scottish Episcopal diocese of Moray, Ross & Caithness, who gifted it to Bishop Robert Eden, the founder of Inverness Cathedral. It was originally known as Eden Court until 1976 when the modern-day Eden Court was built and its name was changed to Bishop's Palace. The house was lived in by bishops until 1947 when Bishop Piers Holt Wilson left the building to live in a smaller, more comfortable house on Fairfield Road. Bishop's Palace received a thorough restoration in 2007 when Eden Court was extended.

Eden Court was extended in 2007 to accommodate a second theatre, two cinemas, two dance and drama studios and three floors of dressing rooms. Nineteenth, 20th and 21st-century buildings combine to make Eden Court what it is today.

Hootananny

Hootananny on Church Street is an award winning bar/restaurant where you'll find live Scottish music and a fine selection of local ales and malt whisky.

The Ironworks

Another treat for music lovers can be found at the bottom of Academy Street. The Ironworks is a purpose-built live music venue capable of attracting big-name acts to the city.

Inverness Caledonian Thistle

In 1994 two of Inverness's great football teams merged to create Caledonian Thistle. Inverness was added to the already lengthy name two years later at the request of the Inverness District Council. Both teams, up to this point, had competed in the semi-professional Highland League. Caledonian and Inverness Thistle were clubs steeped in history and as bitter rivals their amalgamation caused some fierce debate among their loyal fans. For many years Inverness football supporters had made calls for a team from the Highland capital to compete alongside Scotland's elite footballing sides and this at last became a reality in 1994 when a vacancy in the Scottish Football League became available. Over the next 10 years a fairytale rise through the ranks of Scottish football would ensue, and along the way they became known as giant-killers due to many great results against seemingly superior opposition. The most famous of these victories came in February 2000, when the Highland capital side overcame the might of Glasgow Celtic by three goals to one at Celtic Park while being a division below their illustrious opponents. Inverness Caledonian Thistle's 10th anniversary saw them promoted to Scotland's top flight – the Scottish Premier League. Not even the most optimistic supporter could have believed that this would be possible in such a short space of time. However, there was still one obstacle to clear: the Scottish Premier League dictated that to compete in the top tier, football clubs must have an all-seater stadium with a minimum of 6,000 seats. Caledonian Stadium was well short of that figure, and so began the incredibly swift erection of two stands, carried out by Tulloch Construction in just 47 days. In the meantime Inverness CT ground-shared with Aberdeen FC, returning to their completed stadium halfway through their first SPL season. From its humble beginnings, Inverness Caledonian Thistle has shown that almost anything is possible, while no doubt helping to put the city of Inverness firmly on the map.

The Tulloch Caledonian Stadium was built in 1996. Between 1994 and 1996 Inverness Caledonian Thistle played at Inverness Caledonian's Telford Street Stadium.

The main entrance to the Tulloch Caledonian Stadium.

The highly anticipated local derby between Inverness Caledonian Thistle and Dingwall side Ross County usually draws a large crowd.

Former Inverness Caledonian Thistle player Richie Hart is swarmed by fans as he celebrates with the Scottish First Division Trophy.

The North Stand is one of the two stands that were rapidly added to the stadium following Inverness Caledonian Thistle's promotion.

The Black Isle is neither black, nor is it an island. It is in fact a peninsula, which can be found by heading north over the Kessock Bridge from Inverness. Around 90 per cent of the Black Isle is surrounded by water that is made up of the Cromarty, Moray and Beauly Firths. Situated next to the Kessock Bridge is the village of North Kessock, which is an excellent point from which to try and catch a glimpse of the Moray Firth dolphins.

Surrounding Area

Inverness is fortunate enough to be situated among some of Scotland's finest scenery and as a small city you don't have to travel far from the centre to find it. The landscape surrounding Inverness can boast an abundance of mountains, lochs, and woodland.

The Black Isle is blessed with some lovely coastal villages including Avoch, which is situated on its southern coastline. Dolphin and seal-spotting boat trips sail from Avoch Harbour during the summer months.

Black Isle
A view of the Beauly Firth from North Kessock.

Not far from Avoch is Fortrose, where the ruins of a 13th-century cathedral can be found. Fortrose Cathedral was used as the town church up until the Reformation in 1560 when the cathedral lost its status and became obsolete. In the 1650s stone from the building was used to construct Cromwell's citadel in Inverness.

Fortrose is also home to the Gothic-styled St Andrew's Episcopal Church, which was built in 1827.

Less than a mile from Fortrose is the village of Rosemarkie, where a fine-looking sandy beach can be found.

Chanonry Point is a spit of land that stretches over a mile from Fortrose and Rosemarkie into the Moray Firth.

The lighthouse at Chanonry Point was built by famous lighthouse engineer Alan Stevenson in 1846. The Moray Firth's narrowest point east of Inverness can be found between the peninsulas of Fort George and Chanonry Point.

Chanonry Point is regarded as one of the best spots in the UK to view Bottlenose Dolphins. Swimming in pods, the dolphins, which can grow up to four metres in length, feed on fish in the Moray Firth. They can be seen only metres from the shore at Chanonry Point as they put on a show for the gathering crowds.

This stone at Chanonry Point commemorates the legend of the Brahan Seer. The Brahan Seer was a 17th-century Highland prophet who is said to have predicted, among other things, the invention of television, the Battle of Culloden, the building of the Caledonian Canal and the discovery of oil in the North Sea. He worked as a labourer for the Seaforth family at Brahan Castle near Dingwall. During his time there Lady Seaforth, wife of the 3rd Earl of Seaforth, asked the Brahan Seer for news on her husband who was away in Paris. The prophet envisaged the Earl's infidelity with a French woman but simply told her that the Earl was well. When Lady Seaforth demanded that he tell her more the Brahan Seer reluctantly told her the truth, which is said to have led to him being burnt alive in a barrel of boiling tar at Chanonry Point.

Ben Wyvis (seen here in the background) can be found north-west of the Black Isle in Easter Ross. The 1,046m (3,432ft) Munro (the name given to any mountain over 3,000ft in Scotland) can be seen from Inverness, which is around 20 miles away.

Lochs

To the south-west of Inverness is a group of lochs that run parallel to Loch Ness. The first of these is Loch Ashie, which along with Loch Duntelchaig provides Inverness with its water supply.

Water from Loch Duntelchaig is fed via a water pump to Loch Ashie where it is then gravity-fed towards Inverness.

A drive along the southern shores of Loch Duntelchaig leads to Loch Ruthven, where a nature reserve can be found. Bird lovers will enjoy catching a glimpse of the Slavonian grebe, which can be found at Loch Ruthven in early spring.

Loch Ceo Glais is situated half a mile south-west of Loch Duntelchaig – the loch into which it drains.

Around 10 miles or so south of Inverness lies the serene Loch Farr. There are some lovely forest walks to be had here and some excellent picnic spots dotted around the loch's shores.

Loch Mhor is a large loch located about five miles south-west of Loch Ceo Glais. Loch Mhor is made up of two smaller lochs (Loch Garth and Loch Farraline), which were joined in 1896 to provide a reservoir for the British Aluminium Company at Foyers.

Loch Mhor reservoir is now used as part of Foyers' hydro-electric power scheme. During the day water from Loch Mhor generates electricity as it is gravity-fed via tunnels to Foyers Power Station. Then at night, when demand for electricity is low, it is pumped back up to Loch Mhor ready to repeat the process the following day.

Castle Stuart

Castle Stuart lies several miles east of Inverness. It was built in 1625 by James Stuart, 3rd Earl of Moray, and is famed for being one the most haunted castles in Scotland.

Highland Cow

Highland cows like this one are a common sight in the area surrounding Inverness.

Inverness Airport

Inverness Airport can be found around eight miles north-east of the city centre at Dalcross. The airport has a small but modern terminal which deals with over half a million passengers annually.

This statue of Captain Ernest Edmund Fresson, OBE, who pioneered aviation in the north of Scotland by establishing Highland Airways, stands at the entrance to Inverness Airport. In 1933 Fresson began flying scheduled flights from Longman Aerodrome in Inverness to Wick and Kirkwall.

Cawdor Castle

Cawdor Castle can be found roughly 12 miles from Inverness. Documentation states that the castle was built by the Thanes of Cawdor in 1454, although some architectural historians believe that the oldest parts of the castle may actually date back to 1380.

The castle, which to this day is lived in by the Cawdor family, is open to the public from May to October.

Cawdor Castle is surrounded by beautifully kept gardens, nature trails and a nine-hole golf course.

About 16 miles east of Inverness is the attractive seaside town of Nairn, which has been a popular holiday destination since Victorian times. A trip to Nairn makes a great family day out with putting greens, and a beachside children's play area. Two golf courses and miles of sandy coastline are among the many attractions.

Cairngorms

No visit to the Highland capital would be complete with a trip to the Cairngorm National Park, where mountains, lochs and ancient woodland make up 1,400 square miles of almost unspoilt parkland.

The Cairngorms can be found roughly 30 miles south of Inverness. Around 20 miles into your journey look out for the 'German Soldier's Head', which will be on your left as you travel south on the A9. It is a natural rock formation that has taken on the shape of a head wearing a German soldier's helmet. It's easy to miss as it isn't signposted, so only passengers should partake in trying to spot it.

The village of Carrbridge can be found 23 miles south of Inverness. The village is named after its most notable feature – an old packhorse bridge (seen here). Built in 1717, the bridge crosses the River Dulnain, which flooded in 1829 leaving the bridge in the ruinous state we see today. Carrbridge is also home to Landmark Forest Adventure Park, which makes a fun-filled day out for all the family.

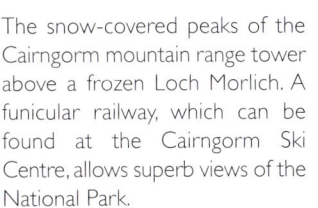

From Carrbridge continue on your journey south towards Aviemore where you may want to stop for something to eat before heading for Loch Morlich (seen here).

Loch Morlich lies in the heart of Cairngorm National Park. Loch Morlich and the Cairngorms offer the outdoor enthusiast a wide range of activities including hillwalking, cycling, fishing, watersports and skiing.

The snow-covered peaks of the Cairngorm mountain range tower above a frozen Loch Morlich. A funicular railway, which can be found at the Cairngorm Ski Centre, allows superb views of the National Park.

Four miles west of Loch Morlich lies Loch An Eilean, where the ruins of a 13th-century island castle can be found. The castle, which was once connected to the shore by a causeway, is thought to have been built by Alexander Stewart, the notorious Wolf of Badenoch. Although the ruined castle hasn't seen much human activity in recent times, it does provide shelter for the ospreys that today nest within its walls. Loch An Eilean also has some excellent woodland paths which can be enjoyed by walkers and cyclists.

Around 10 miles north-east of Loch An Eilean, Loch Garten can be found. Ospreys have made the ancient Caledonian pinewood which surrounds Loch Garten their home. It is possible to view the ospreys via CCTV from an RSPB hide at Loch Garten.

Aurora Borealis
The spectacular natural light display that is the Aurora Borealis (Northern Lights) can be viewed on occasion from Inverness. This image was captured from the United Kingdom's most northerly city in October 2003.